Ruby M Grimes
Apr. 7 - '71

Books by James Whitcomb Riley

NEGHBORLY POEMS

SKETCHES IN PROSE, WITH INTERLUDING VERSES

AFTERWHILES

PIPES O' PAN (Prose and Verse)

RHYMES OF CHILDHOOD

FLYING ISLANDS OF THE NIGHT

GREEN FIELDS AND RUNNING BROOKS

ARMAZINDY

A CHILD-WORLD

HOME FOLKS

HIS PA'S ROMANCE

(The volumes above are bound in a uniform set known as the Greenfield edition)

OLD-FASHIONED ROSES

THE GOLDEN YEAR

POEMS HERE AT HOME

RUBÁIYÁT OF DOC SIFERS

THE BOOK OF JOYOUS CHILDREN

RILEY CHILD-RHYMES (With Hoosier Pictures)

RILEY LOVE-LYRICS (Pictures by Dyer)

RILEY FARM-RHYMES (Pictures by Vawter)

AN OLD SWEETHEART OF MINE (Pictures by Christy)

JAMES WHITCOMB RILEY

His Pa's Romance

James Whitcomb Riley

With Illustrations by
Will Vawter and a Portrait by
John Cecil Clay

Indianapolis
The Bobbs-Merrill Company
Publishers

NOVEMBER

PRESS OF
BRAUNWORTH & CO.
BOOKBINDERS AND PRINTERS
BROOKLYN, N. Y.

His Pa's Romance

TO—

EDGAR WILSON NYE

SUCH *silence—after such glad merriment!*
O prince of halest humor, wit and cheer;
Could you speak yet to us, I doubt not we
Should catch your voice, still blithely eloquent
Above all murmurings of sorrow here,
Calling your love back to us laughingly.

Contents

CONTENTS

His Pa's Romance

HIS PA'S ROMANCE

All 'at I ever want to be
Is ist to be a man like Pa
When he wuz young an' married Ma!
Uncle he telled us yisterdy
Ist all about it then—'cause they,
My Pa an' Ma, wuz bofe away
To 'tend P'tracted Meetin', where
My Pa an' Ma is allus there
When all the big "Revivals" is,
An' "Love-Feasts," too, an' "Class," an'
"Prayer,"
An' when's "Comoonian Servicis."
An', yes, an' Uncle said to not
To never tell *them* nor let on
Like we knowed now ist how they got
First married. So—while they wuz gone—

Uncle he telled us ever'thing—
'Bout how my Pa wuz ist a pore
Farm-boy.—He says, I tell you *what,*
Your Pa wuz pore! But neighbors they
All liked him—all but one old man
An' his old wife that folks all say
Nobody liked, ner never can!
Yes, sir! an' Uncle purt'-nigh swore
About the mean old man an' way
He treat' my Pa!—'cause he's a pore
Farm-hand—but prouder 'an a king—
An' ist work' on, he did, an' wore
His old patched clo'es, ist anyway,
So he saved up his wages—then
He ist worked on an' saved some more,
An' ist worked on, ist night an' day—
Till, sir, he save' up nine or ten
Er hunnerd dollars! But he keep
All still about it, Uncle say—
But he ist thinks—an' thinks a heap!
Though what he wuz a-thinkin', Pa

He never tell' a soul but Ma—
(Then, course, you know, he wuzn't Pa,
An', course, you know, she wuzn't Ma—
They wuz ist sweethearts, course you know) ;
'Cause Ma wuz ist a girl, about
Sixteen ; an' when my Pa he go
A-courtin' her, her Pa an' Ma—
The very first they find it out—
Wuz maddest folks you ever saw !
'Cause it wuz her old Ma an' Pa
'At hate' my Pa, an' toss their head,
An' ist raise Ned ! An' her Pa said
He'd ruther see his daughter dead !
An' said she's ist a child !—an' so
Wuz Pa !—An' ef he wuz man-grown
An' only man on earth below,
His daughter shouldn't marry him
Ef he's a king an' on his throne !
Pa's chances then looked mighty slim
Fer certain, Uncle said. But he—

He never told a soul but her
What he wuz keepin' quiet fer.

Her folks ist lived a mile from where
He lived at—an' they drove past there

To git to town. An' ever' one
An' all the neighbors they liked her
An' showed it! But her folks—no, sir!—
Nobody liked her parents none!
An' so when they shet down, you know,
On Pa—an' old man tell' him so—
Pa ist went back to work, an' she
Ist waited. An', sir! purty soon
Her folks they thought he's turned his eye
Some other way—'cause by-an'-by
They heerd he'd *rented* the old place
He worked on. An' one afternoon
A neighbor, that had bust' a trace,
He tell' the old man they wuz signs
Around the old place that the young
Man wuz a-fixin' up the old
Log cabin some, an' he had brung
New furnichur from town; an' told
How th' old house 'uz whitewashed clean
An' sweet—wiv mornin'-glory vines
An' hollyhawks all 'round the door

An' winders—an' a bran'-new floor
In th' old porch—an' wite-new green-
An'-red pump in the old sweep-well!
An', Uncle said, when he hear tell
O' all them things, the old man he
Ist grin' an' says, he "reckon' now
Some gal, er widder anyhow,
That silly boy he's coaxed at last
To marry him!" he says, says-ee,
"An' ef he has, 'so mote it be'!"
Then went back to the house to tell
His *wife* the news, as he went past
The smokehouse, an' then went on in
The kitchen, where his daughter she
Wuz washin', to tell *her,* an' grin
An' try to worry her a spell!
The mean old thing! But Uncle said
She ain't cry much—ist pull her old
Sunbonnet forrerds on her head—
So's old man he can't see her face
At all! An' when he s'pose he scold'

An' jaw enough, he ist clear' out
An' think he's boss of all the place!

Then Uncle say, the first you know
They's go' to be a Circus-show

In town; an' old man think he'll take
His wife an' go. An' when she say
To take their daughter, too, *she* shake
Her head like she don't *want* to go;
An' when he sees she wants to stay,

The old man takes her, anyway!
An' so she went! But Uncle he
Said she looked mighty sweet that day,
Though she wuz pale as she could be,
A-speshully a-drivin' by
Wite where her beau lived at, you know;
But out the corner of his eye
The old man watch' her; but she throw
He pairsol 'round so she can't see
The house at all! An' then she hear
Her Pa an' Ma a-talkin' low
An' kindo' laughin'-like; but she
Ist set there in the seat behind,
P'tendin' like she didn't mind.
An', Uncle say, when they got past
The young man's place, an' 'pearantly
He wuzn't home, but off an' gone
To town, the old man turned at last
An' talked back to his daughter there,
All pleasant-like, from then clean on
Till they got into town, an' where

The Circus wuz, an' on inside
O' that, an' through the crowd, on to

The very top seat in the tent
Wite next the band—a-bangin' through
A tune 'at bust his yeers in two!

An' there the old man scrouged an' tried
To make his wife set down, an' she
A-yellin'! But ist what she meant
He couldn't hear, ner couldn't see
Till she turned 'round an' pinted. Then
He turned an' looked—an' looked again! . .
He ist saw neighbors ever'where—
But, sir, *his daughter* wuzn't there!
An', Uncle says, he even saw
Her beau, you know, he hated so;
An' he wuz with some other girl.
An' then he heerd the Clown "Haw-haw!"
An' saw the horses wheel an' whirl
Around the ring, an' heerd the zipp
O' the Ringmaster's long slim whip—
But that whole Circus, Uncle said,
Wuz all inside the old man's head!

An' Uncle said, he didn't find
His daughter all that afternoon—
An' her Ma says she'll lose her mind

Ef they don't find her purty soon!
But, though they looked all day, an' stayed
There fer the night p'formance—not
No use at all!—they never laid
Their eyes on her. An' then they got
Their team out, an' the old man shook
His fist at all the town, an' then
Shook it up at the moon ag'in,
An' said his time 'ud come, some day!
An' jerked the lines an' driv away.

Uncle, he said, he 'spect, that night,
The old man's madder yet when they
Drive past the young man's place, an' hear
A fiddle there, an' see a light
Inside, an' shadders light an' gay
A-dancin' 'crost the winder-blinds.
An' some young chaps outside yelled, "Say!
What 'pears to be the hurry—hey?"
But the old man ist whipped the lines
An' streaked past like a runaway!

An' now you'll be su'prised, I bet!—
I hardly ain't quit laughin' yet
When Uncle say, that jamboree
An' dance an' all—w'y, that's a sign
That any old man ort to see,
As plain as 8 and 1 makes 9,
That they's a weddin' wite inside
That very house he's whippin' so
To git apast—an', sir! the bride
There's his own daughter! Yes, an' oh!
She's my Ma now—an' young man she
Got married, he's my Pa! Whoop-ee!
But Uncle say to not laugh all
The laughin' yet, but please save some
To kindo' spice up what's to come!

Then Uncle say, about next day
The neighbers they begin to call
An' wish 'em well, an' say how glad
An' proud an' tickled ever' way
Their friends all is—an' how they had

The lovin' prayers of ever' one
That had homes of their own! But none
Said nothin' 'bout the home that she
Had run away from! So she sighed
Sometimes—an' wunst she purt'-nigh cried.

Well, Uncle say, her old Pa, he
Ist like to died, he wuz so mad!
An' her Ma, too! But by-an'-by
They cool down some.

An', 'bout a week,
She want to see her Ma so bad,
She think she'll haf to go! An' so
She coax him; an' he kiss her cheek
An' say, Lord bless her, *course* they'll go!
An', Uncle say, when they're bofe come
A-knockin' there at her old home—
W'y, first he know, the door it flew
Open, all quick, an' she's jerked in,
An', quicker still, the door's banged to
An' locked: an' crosst the winder-sill

The old man pokes a shotgun through
An' says to git! "You stold my child,"

He says; "an', now she's back, w'y you
Clear out, this minute, er I'll kill

You! Yes, an' I 'ull kill her, too,
Ef you don't go!" An' then, all wild,
His young wife begs him please to go!
An' so he turn' an' walk'—all slow
An' pale as death, but awful still
An' ca'm—back to the gate, an' on
Into the road, where he had gone
So many times alone, you know!
An', Uncle say, a whipperwill
Holler so lonesome, as he go
On back to'rds home, he say he 'spec'
He ist 'ud like to wring its neck!
An' I ain't think he's goin' back
All by hisse'f—but Uncle say
That's what he does, an' it's a fac'!

An' 'pears-like he's gone back to stay—
'Cause there he stick', ist thataway,
An' don't go nowheres any more,
Ner don't nobody ever see

Him set his foot outside the door—
Till 'bout five days, a boy loped down
The road, a-comin' past from town,
An' he called to him from the gate,

An' sent the old man word: He's thought
Things over now; an', while he hate
To lose his wife, he think she ought
To mind her Pa an' Ma an' do

Whatever *they* advise her to.
An' sends word, too, to come an' git
Her new things an' the furnichur
That he had special' bought fer her—
'Cause, now that they wuz goin' to quit,
She's free to ist have all of it;—
So, fer his love fer her, he say
To come an' git it, wite away.
An' spang! that very afternoon,
Here come her Ma—ist 'bout as soon
As old man could hitch up an' tell
Her "hurry back!" An' 'bout as quick
As she's drove there to where my Pa—
I mean to where her son-in-law—
Lives at, he meets her at the door
All smilin', though he's awful pale
An' trimbly—like he's ist been sick;
He take her in the house—an', 'fore
She knows it, they's a cellar-door
Shet on her, an' she hears the click

Of a' old rusty padlock! Then,
Uncle, he say, she kindo' stands
An' thinks—an' thinks—an' thinks ag'in—
An' maybe thinks of her own child
Locked up—like her! An' Uncle smiled,
An' I ist laughed an' clapped my hands!

An' there she stayed! An' she can cry
Ist all she want! an' yell an' kick
To ist her heart's content! an' try

To pry out wiv a quiltin'-stick!
But Uncle say he guess at last
She 'bout give up, an' holler' through
The door-crack fer to please to be
So kind an' good as send an' tell
The old man, like she want him to,
To come, 'fore night, an' set her free,
Er—they wuz rats down there! An' yell
She did, till, Uncle say, it saured
The morning's milk in the back yard!
But all the answer reached her, where
She's skeerd so in the dark down there,
Wuz ist a mutterin' that she heard—
"I've sent him word!—I've sent him word!"
An' shore enough, as Uncle say,
He *has* "sent word!"

Well, it's plum night
An' all the house is shet up tight—
Only one winder 'bout half-way
Raised up, you know; an' ain't no light
Inside the whole house, Uncle say.

Then, first you know, there where the team
Stands hitched yet, there the old man
stands—
A' old tin lantern in his hands
An' monkey-wrench; an' he don't seem
To make things out, a-standin' there.
He comes on to the gate an' feels
An' fumbles fer the latch—then hears
A voice that chills him to the heels—
"You halt! an' stand right where you air!"
Then, sir! my—my—his son-in-law,
There at the winder wiv his gun,
He tell the old man what he's done:
"You hold *my* wife a prisoner—
An' *your* wife, drat ye! I've got *her!*
An' now, sir," Uncle say he say,
"You ist turn round an' climb wite in
That wagon, an' drive home ag'in
An' bring my wife back wite away,
An' we'll trade then—an' not before
Will I unlock my cellar-door—

Not fer your wife's sake ner your own,
But *my* wife's sake—an' her's alone!"

An', Uncle say, it don't sound like
It's so, but yet it is!—He say,

From wite then, somepin' seem' to strike
The old man's funny-bone some way;
An', minute more, that team o' his
Went tearin' down the road k'whiz!
An' in the same two-forty style
Come whizzin' back! An' oh, that-air
Sweet girl a-cryin' all the while,
Thinkin' about her Ma there, shet
In her own daughter's cellar, where
Ist week or so *she's* kep' house there,
She hadn't time to clean it yet!
So when her Pa an' her they git
There—an' the young man grab' an' kiss
An' hug her, till she make him quit
An' ask him where her mother is.
An' then he smile' an' try to not;
Then slow-like find th' old padlock key,
An' blow a' oat-hull out of it,
An' then stoop down there where he's got
Her Ma locked up so keerfully—
An' where, wite there, he say he thought

It *ort* to been *the old man*—though
Uncle, he say, he reckon not—
When out she bounced, all tickled so
To taste fresh air ag'in an' find
Her folks wunst more, an' grab' her child
An' cry an' laugh, an' even go
An' hug the old man; an' he wind

Her in his arms, an' laugh, an' pat
Her back, an' say he's riconciled,
In such a happy scene as that,
To swop his daughter for her Ma,
An' have so smart a son-in-law
As *they* had! "Yes, an' he's my Pa!"
I laugh' an' yell', "Hooray-hooraw!"

TWILIGHT STORIES

NEITHER *daylight, starlight, moonlight,*
But a sad-sweet term of some light
By the saintly name of Twilight.

The Grandma Twilight Stories!—Still,
  A childish listener, I hear
The katydid and whippoorwill,
  In deepening atmosphere

Of velvet dusk, blent with the low
  Soft music of the voice that sings
And tells me tales of long ago
  And old enchanted things. . . .

While far fails the last dim daylight,
And the fireflies in the Twilight
Drift about like flakes of starlight.

ALMOST BEYOND ENDURANCE

I AIN'T a-goin' to cry no more, no more!
I'm got ear-ache, an' Ma can't make
It quit a-tall;
An' Carlo bite my rubber-ball
An' puncture it; an' Sis she take
An' poke' my knife down through the stable-floor
An' loozed it—blame it all!
But I ain't goin' to cry no more, no more!

An' Aunt Mame *wrote* she's comin', an' she *can't*—
Folks is come *there!*—An' I don't care
She *is* my Aunt!
An' my eyes stings; an' I'm
Ist coughin' all the time,

An' hurts me so, an' where my side's so sore
Grampa felt where, an' he
Says "Mayby it's *pleurasy!*"
But I ain't goin' to cry no more, no more!

An' I clumbed up an' nen falled off the fence,
An' Herbert he ist laugh at me!
An' my fi'-cents

It sticked in my tin bank, an' I ist tore
Purt'-nigh my thumbnail off, a-tryin' to git
It out—nen *smash* it!—An' it's in there yit!
But I ain't goin' to cry no more, no more!

Oo! I'm so wickud!—An' my breath's so *hot*—
Ist like I run an' don't res' none
But ist run on when I ought to not;
Yes, an' my chin
An' lips 's all warpy, an' teeth's so fast,
An' 's a place in my throat I can't swaller
past—
An' they all hurt so!—
An' oh, my-oh!
I'm a-startin' ag'in—
I'm a-*startin'* ag'in, but I *won't,* fer shore!—
I ist ain't goin' to cry no more, no more!

A SIMPLE RECIPE

To be a wholly worthy man,
  As you, my boy, would like to be,—
This is to show you how you can—
  This simple recipe:—

Be honest—both in word and act,
  Be strictly truthful through and through:
Fact cannot fail.—You stick to fact,
  And fact will stick to you.
Be clean—outside and in, and sweep
  Both hearth and heart and hold them bright;
Wear snowy linen—aye, and keep
  Your conscience snowy-white.

Do right, your utmost—good *must* come
  To you who do your level best—
Your very hopes will help you some,
  And work will do the rest.

THE LISPER

ELSIE MINGUS *lisps,* she does!
She lives wite acrosst from us
  In Miz. Ayers'uz house 'at she
Rents part to the Mingusuz.—
  Yes, an' Elsie plays wiv me.

Elsie lisps so, she can't say
Her own name, ist *anyway!*—

She says *"Elthy"*—like they wuz
Feathers on her words, an' they
Ist stick on her tongue like fuzz.

My! she 's *purty,* though!—An' when
She *lisps,* w'y, she 's purty *nen!*
When she telled me, wunst, her doll
Wuz so "thweet," an' I p'ten'
I lisp too,—she laugh'—'at 's all!—

She don't never git mad none—
'Cause she know I'm ist in fun.—
Elsie she ain't one bit sp'iled.—
Of all childerns—ever' one—
She's the *ladylikest* child!—

My Ma *say* she is! One time
Elsie start to say the rhyme,
"Thing a thong o' thixpenth"—*Whee!*
I ist *yell!* An' Ma say I'm
Unpolite as I can be!

Wunst I went wiv Ma to call
On Elsie's Ma, an' eat an' all;
  An' nen Elsie, when we've et,
An' we 're playin' in the hall,
  Elsie say: It 's etikett

Fer young gentlemens, like me,
Eatin' when they 's *company*,
  Not to never ever crowd
Down their food, ner "thip their tea
  Ner thup thoop so awful loud!"

OUR BETSY

Us childern 's all so lonesome,
We hardly want to *play*
Or skip or swing or anything,—
'Cause Betsy she's away!

She's gone to see her people
At her old home.—But then—
Oh! every child 'll jist be wild
When she's back here again!

CHORUS

Then it 's whoopty-doopty dooden!—
Whoopty-dooden then!
Oh! it 's whoopty-doopty dooden,
When Betsy 's back again!

She's like a mother to us,
And like a sister, too—
Oh! she's as sweet as things to eat
When all the dinner 's through!

And hey! to hear her laughin'!
And ho! to hear her sing!—
To have her back is all we lack
Of havin' *everything!*

CHORUS

Then it 's whoopty-doopty dooden!—
Whoopty-dooden then!
Oh! it 's whoopty-doopty dooden,
When Betsy 's back again!

Oh! some may sail the northern lakes,
  And some to foreign lands,
And some may seek old Nameless Creek,
  Or India's golden sands;

Or some may go to Kokomo,
  And some to Mackinac,—
But I'll go down to Morgantown
  To fetch our Betsy back.

CHORUS

Then it 's whoopty-doopty dooden!—
  Whoopty-dooden then!
Oh! it 's whoopty-doopty dooden,
  When Betsy 's back again!

THE TOY-BALLOON

They wuz a Big Day wunst in town,
An' little Jason's Pa
Buyed him a little toy-balloon,
The first he ever saw.—
An' oh! but Jase wuz *more'n* proud,
A-holdin' to the string
An' scrougin' through the grea'-big crowd,
To hear the Glee Club sing.

The Glee Club it wuz goin' to sing
In old Masonic Hall;
An' Speakin', it wuz in there, too,
An' soldiers, folks an' all:
An' Jason's Pa he git a seat
An' set down purty soon,
A-holdin' little Jase, an' him
A-holdin' his balloon.

An' while the Speakin' 's startin' up
  An' ever'body still—
The first you know wuz little Jase
  A-yellin' fit to kill!—
Nen Jason's Pa jump on his seat
  An' grab up in the air,—
But little Jason's toy-balloon
  Wuz clean away from there!

An' Jase he yelled; an' Jase's Pa,
  Still lookin' up, clumb down—
While that-air little toy-balloon
  Went bumpin' roun' an' roun'
Ag'inst the ceilin', 'way up there
  Where ever'body saw,
An' *they* all yelled, an' *Jason* yelled,
  An' little Jason's Pa!

But when his Pa he packed him out
  A-screamin'—nen the crowd
Looked down an' hushed—till they looked up
  An' howled again out loud;

An' nen the speaker, mad an' pale,
  Jist turned an' left the stand,
An' all j'ined in the Glee Club—"Hail,
  Columby, Happy Land!"

SOME CHRISTMAS YOUNGSTERS

I

THE STRENGTH OF THE WEAK

LAST Chris'mus, little Benny
  Wuzn't sick so bad,—
Now he 's had the worst spell
  Ever yet he had.
Ever' Chris'mus-morning, though,
  He 'll p'tend as if
He 's asleep—an' first you know
  He 's got your "Chris'mus-gif'!"

Pa he 's good to *all* of us
  All the time; but when,
Ever' time it 's *Chris'mus,*
  He's as good again!—

'Sides our toys an' candy,
  Ever' Chris'mus, he
Gives us all a quarter,
  Certain as can be!

Pa, this morning, tiptoe' in
  To make the fire, you know,
Long 'fore it 's daylight,
  An' all 's ice an' snow!—

An' Benny holler, *"Chris'mus-gif'!"*
  An' Pa jump an' say,
"You 'll only git a *dollar* if
  You skeer me thataway!"

II

THE LITTLE QUESTIONER

BABE she 's so always
  Wantin' more to hear
All about Santy Claus,
  An' says: "Mommy dear,
Where 's Santy's *home* at
  When he ain't *away?*—
An' is they *Mizzus* Santy Claus
  An' *little folks*—say?—
Chris'mus, Santy 's always *here*—
  Don't *they* want him, too?
When it *ain't* Chris'mus
  What does he do?"

III

PARENTAL CHRISTMAS PRESENTS

PARUNTS don't git toys an' things,
  Like you 'd think they *ruther.*—
Mighty funny Chris'mus-gif's
  Parunts gives each other!—
Pa give Ma a barrel o' flour.
  An' Ma she give to Pa
The nicest dinin'-table
  She know he ever saw!

OLD GRANNY DUSK

Old Granny Dusk, when the sun goes down,
Here *she* comes into thish-yer town!
Out o' the wet black woods an' swamps
In she traipses an' trails an' tromps—
With her old sunbonnet all floppy an' brown,
An' her cluckety shoes, an' her old black gown,
Here *she* comes into thish-yer town!

Old Granny Dusk, when the bats begin
To flap around, comes a-trompin' in!
An' the katydids they rasp an' whir,
An' the lightnin'-bugs all blink at *her;*
An' the old Hop-toad turns in his thumbs,
An' the bunglin' June-bug booms an' bums,
An' the Bullfrog croaks, "O here *she* comes!"

Old Granny Dusk, though I'm 'feard o' you,
Shore-fer-certain I'm sorry, too:
'Cause you look as lonesome an' starved an' sad
As a mother 'at's lost ever' child she had.—
Yet never a child in thish-yer town
Clings at yer hand er yer old black gown,
Er kisses the face you 're a-bendin' down.

THE YOUNG OLD MAN

VOLUNTARY BY ARTLESS "LITTLE BROTHER"

MAMMA is a widow: there's only us three—
Our pretty Mamma, little sister, and me:
And we 've come to live in this new neighborhood
Where all seems so quiet, old-fashioned and good.
Mamma sits and sews at the window, and I—
I 'm out at the gate when an old man goes by—
Such a *lovely* old man,—though I can't tell you why,
Unless it's his greeting,—"Good morning!
Good morning! good morning!" the old man will say,—
"Fine bracing weather we're having to-day!—

And how 's little brother—
And sister—and mother?—
So dear to each other!—
Good morning!"

The old man goes by, in his glossy high-hat,
And stripe-trousers creased, and all turned-up, at
that,
And his glancing nose-glasses—and pleasantest
eyes,
As he smiles on me, always in newer surprise:
And though his mustache is as white as the
snow,
He wears it waxed out and all pointed, you
know,
And gloves, and high collar and bright, jaunty
bow,
And stylish umbrella.—"Good morning!

Good morning! good morning!" the old man
will say,—
"Fine falling weather we're promised to-
day!—
And how 's little brother—
And sister—and mother?—
So fond of each other!—
Good morning!"

. . . .

It's Christmas!—it's Christmas! and oh, but
we're gay!
The postman's been here, and Ma says, "Run and
play:—
You must leave your Mamma to herself for a
while!"
And so sweet is her voice, and so tender her
smile!—
And she looks *so* pretty and happy and—
Well!—
She 's just too delicious for language to tell!—

So Sis hugs her *more*—and *I* answer the bell,—
And there in the doorway—"Good morning!—
Good morning! good morning! good morning, I say!—
Fine Christmas weather we're having today!—
And how 's little brother—
Dear sister—er, ruther—
Why, here *is* your *mother*. . . .
Good morning!"

WHEN UNCLE DOC WAS YOUNG

THOUGH Doctor Glenn—the best of men—
  Is wrinkled, old, and gray,
He 'll always smile and stop awhile
  Where little children play:

And often then he tells us, when
He was a youngster, too,
He was as glad and bad a lad
As old folks ever knew!

As he walks down, no boy in town
But sees him half a block,
And stops to shout a welcome out
With "Here comes Uncle Doc!"
Then all the rest, they look their best
As he lines up among
Us boys of ten—each thinking then
When Uncle Doc was young.

We *run* to him!—Though grave and grim,
With voice pitched high and thin,
He still reveals the joy he feels
In all that *he* has been:

With heart too true, and honest, too,
  To ever *hide* a truth,
He frankly owns, in laughing tones,
  He was "a sorry youth!"—

When he was young, he says, he sung
  And howled his level-best;
He says he guyed, and sneaked, and lied,
  And wrecked the robin's nest.—

And this, and worse, will he rehearse,
  Then smooth his snowy locks
And look the saint he says he ain't. . . .
  Them eyes of Uncle Doc's!

He says, when he—like you and me—
  Was just too low and mean
To slap asleep, he used to weep
  To find his face was clean:
His hair, he said, was just too red
  To tell with mortal tongue—
"The Burning Shame" was his nickname
  When Uncle Doc was young.

BILLY MILLER'S CIRCUS-SHOW

At Billy Miller's Circus-Show—
  In their old stable where it's at—
The boys pays twenty pins to go,
  An' gits their money's-worth at that!—

'Cause Billy he can climb and chalk
His stockin'-feet an' purt'-nigh walk
A tight-rope—yes, an' ef he fall
He'll ketch, an' "skin a cat"—'at's all!

He ain't afeard to swing and hang
  Ist by his legs!—an' mayby stop
An' yell "Look out!" an' nen—k-spang!—
  He'll let loose, upside-down, an' drop
  Wite on his hands! An' nen he'll do
  "Contortion-acts"—ist limber through
  As "Injarubber Mens" 'at goes
  With shore-fer-certain circus-shows!

At Billy Miller's Circus-Show
  He's got a circus-ring—an' they's
A dressin'-room,—so's he can go
  An' dress an' paint up when he plays
  He's somepin' else;—'cause sometimes he's
  "Ringmaster"—bossin' like he please—
  An' sometimes "Ephalunt"—er "Bare-
  Back Rider," prancin' out o' there!

An' sometimes—an' the best of all!—
  He's "The Old Clown," an' got on clo'es
All stripud,—an' white hat, all tall
  An' peakud—like in shore-'nuff shows,—

An' got three-cornered red-marks, too,
On his white cheeks—ist like they do!—
An' you'd ist die, the way he sings
An' dances an' says funny things!

THE LAW OF THE PERVERSE

WHERE did the custom come from, anyway?—
  Sending the boys to "play," at dinner-time,
When we have company? What is there, pray,
    About the starched, unmalleable guest
    That, in the host's most genial interest,
Finds *him* first favor on Thanksgiving Day
  Beside the steaming turkey, with its wings
  Akimbo over all the savory things
  It has been stuffed with, yet may never thus
  Make one poor boy's face glad and glorious!

Fancy the exiled boy in the back-yard,
  Ahungered so that any kind of grub
Were welcome, yet with face set stern and hard,
  Hearing the feasters' laugh and mild hubbub,
  And wanting to kill something with a club!—

Intuitively arguing the unjust
Distinction, as he naturally must,—
The guest with all the opportunity,—
The boy with all the appetite! Ah, me!

So is it that when I, a luckless guest,
  Am thus arraigned at banquet, I sit grim
And sullen, eating nothing with a zest,
With smirking features, yet a soul distressed,
  Missing the banished boy and envying him—
Aye, longing for a spatter on my vest
  From his deflecting spoon, and yearning for
  The wild swoop of his lips insatiate, or
  His ever-ravenous, marauding eye
  Fore-eating everything from soup to pie!

CHAIRLEY BURKE

It's Chairley Burke's in town, b'ys! He's down
til "Jamesy's Place,"
Wid a bran'-new shave upon 'um, an' the fhwhus-
kers aff his face;
He's quit the Section Gang last night, an' yez can
chalk it down
There 's goin' to be the divil's toime, sence Chairley Burke's in town.

It's treatin' iv'ry b'y he is, an' poundin' on the bar
Till iv'ry man he's drinkin' wid must shmoke a
foine cigar;
An' Missus Murphy's little Kate, that's comin'
there for beer,
Can't pay wan cint the bucketful, the whilst that
Chairley's here!

He's joompin' oor the tops o' sthools, the both
forninst an' back!
He'll lave yez pick the blessèd flure, an' walk the
straightest crack!
He's liftin' barrels wid his teeth, and singin'
"Garry Owen"
Till all the house be strikin' hands, sence Chairley
Burke's in town.

The Road-Yaird hands comes dhroppin' in, an'
never goin' back;
An' there's two freights upon the switch—the
wan on aither track—
An' Mr. Gearry, from The Shops, he's mad
enough to swear,
An' durst n't spake a word but grin, the whilst
that Chairley's there!
Och! Chairley!—Chairley!—Chairley Burke! ye
divil, wid yer ways
O' dhrivin' all the troubles aff, these dark an'
gloomy days!

Ohone! that it's meself, wid all the griefs I have
 to dhrown,
Must lave me pick to resht a bit, sence Chairley
 Burke's in town!

SONG—THE OLD MAN OF THE SEA

I'm The Old Man of the Sea—I am!—
  And this is my secret pride,
That I have a hundred shapes, all sham,
  And a hundred names besides:
They have named me "Habit," and "Way," forsooth,
  "Capricious," and "Fancy-free";—
But to you, O Youth, I confess the truth,—
  I'm The Old Man of the Sea.

I'm The Old Man of the Sea, yo-ho!
  So lift up a song with me,
As I sit on the throne of your shoulders, alone,
  I'm The Old Man of the Sea.

Crowned with the crown of your noblest thought,
I'm The Old Man of the Sea:
I reign, rule, ruin, and palter not
In my pitiless tyranny:
You, my lad, are my gay Sinbad,
Frisking about, with me
High on the perch I have always had—
I'm The Old Man of the Sea.

I'm The Old Man of the Sea, yo-ho!
So lift up a song with me,
As I sit on the throne of your shoulders, alone,
I'm The Old Man of the Sea.

Tricked in the guise of your best intent,
I am your failures—all—
I am the victories you invent,
And your high resolves that fall:
I am the vow you are breaking now
As the wassail-bowl swings free
And the red guilt flushes your cheek and brow—
I'm The Old Man of the Sea.

I'm The Old Man of the Sea, yo-ho!
So lift up a song with me,
As I sit on the throne of your shoulders, alone,
I'm The Old Man of the Sea.

I am your false dreams of success
  And your mythical future fame—
Your life-long lies, and your soul's distress
  And your slowly-dying shame:
I'm the clattering half of your latest laugh,
  And your tongue's last perfidy—
Your doom, your tomb, and your epitaph . . .
  I'm The Old Man of the Sea.

I'm The Old Man of the Sea, yo-ho!
  So lift up a song with me,
As I sit on the throne of your shoulders, alone,
  I'm The Old Man of the Sea.

AT NINETY IN THE SHADE

Hot weather? Yes; but really not,
Compared with weather twice as hot.
Find comfort, then, in arguing thus,
And you'll pull through victorious!—
For instance, while you gasp and pant
And try to cool yourself—and can't—
With soda, cream and lemonade,
The heat at ninety in the shade,—
Just calmly sit and ponder o'er
These same degrees, with ninety more
On top of them, and so concede
The weather now is cool indeed!
Think—as the perspiration dews
Your fevered brow, and seems to ooze
From out the ends of every hair—
Whole floods of it, with floods to spare—

Think, I repeat, the while the sweat
Pours down your spine—how hotter yet
Just ninety *more* degrees would be,
And bear *this* ninety patiently!
Think—as you mop your brow and hair,
With sticky feelings everywhere—
How ninety more degrees increase

Of heat like this would start the grease;
Or, think, as you exhausted stand,
A wilted "palmleaf" in each hand—
When the thermometer has done
With ease the lap of ninety-one;
O think, I say, what heat might do
At one hundred and eighty-two—
Just twice the heat you now declare,
Complainingly, is hard to bear.
Or, as you watch the mercury
Mount, still elate, one more degree,
And doff your collar and cravat,
And rig a sponge up in your hat,
And ask Tom, Harry, Dick and Jim
If this is hot enough for him—
Consider how the sun would pour
At one hundred and eighty-four—
Just twice the heat that seems to be
Affecting you unpleasantly,
The very hour that you might find
As cool as dew, were you inclined.

But why proceed when none will heed
Advice apportioned to the need?
Hot weather? Yes; but really not,
Compared with weather twice as hot!

GOOD-BYE ER HOWDY-DO

Say good-bye er howdy-do—
What 's the odds betwixt the two?
Comin'—goin'—every day—
Best friends first to go away—
Grasp of hands you 'd ruther hold
Than their weight in solid gold,
Slips their grip while greetin' you.—
Say good-bye er howdy-do?

Howdy-do, and then, good-bye—
Mixes jist like laugh and cry;
Deaths and births, and worst and best,
Tangled their contrariest;
Ev'ry jinglin' weddin'-bell
Skeerin' up some funer'l knell.—
Here's my song, and there's your sigh.—
Howdy-do, and then, good-bye!

Say good-bye er howdy-do—
Jist the same to me and you;
'Taint worth while to make no fuss,
'Cause the job's put up on us!
Some One's runnin' this concern
That's got nothin' else to learn:
If He's willin', we'll pull through—
Say good-bye er howdy-do!

A LOCAL POLITICIAN FROM AWAY BACK

Jedge is good at argyin'—
  No mistake in that!
Most folks 'at tackles *him*
  He'll skin 'em like a cat!
You see, the Jedge is read up,
  And ben in politics,
Hand-in-glove, you might say,
  Sense back in '56.

Elected to the Shurrif, first,
  Then elected Clerk;
Went into lawin' then,
  And buckled down to work;

Practiced three or four terms,
  Then he run for jedge—
Speechified a little 'round,
  And went in like a wedge!

Run fer Legislatur' twic't—
  Made her, ever' pop!
Keeps on the way he's doin',
  Don't know where he'll stop!
Some thinks he's got his eye
  On the govnership;—
Well, ef he tuk the track,
  Guess he'd make the trip!

But I started out to tell you—
  (Now I allus liked *the man*—
Not fer his politics,
  But *social'*, understan'!—
Fer, 's regards to *my* views,
  Political and sich,—
When we come together there
  We're purty ap' to hitch.)

Ketched him in at Knox's shop
  On'y t'other day—
Gittin' shaved, the Jedge was,
  Er somepin' thataway.—
Well, I tetched him up some
  On the silver bill:—
Jedge says, "I won't discuss it;"
  I says, "You *will!*"

I-says-ee, "I reckon
  You'll concede with me,
Coin's the on'y ginuine
  Money," I-says-ee;

Says I, "What's a dollar-bill?"
  Says I, "What's a ten—
Er forty-leven hunderd of 'em?—
  Give us specie, then!"

I seed I was a gittin'
  The Jedge kindo' red
Around the gills. He hawked some
  And cle'red his throat and said!—
"Facts is too complicated
  'Bout the bill in view,"
Squirmed and told the barber then
  He wisht he'd hurry through.

'Ll, then, I knowed I had him,—
  And the crowd around the fire
Was all a-winkin' at me,
  As the barber raised him higher—
Says I, "Jedge, what's a dollar?—
  Er a half-un," I-says-ee—
"What's a *quarter?*—What's a *dime?*"
  "What's *cents?*" says he.

W'y I had him fairly b'ilin'!
  "You needn't comb my hair,"
He says to the barber—
  "I want fresh air;"
And you'd a-died a-laughin'
  To a-seed him grab his hat,
As I-says-ee, says I, "Jedge,
  Where you goin' at!"

Jedge is good at argyin'
  By-and-large; and yit
Beat him at his own game
  And he's goin' to git!
And yit the Jedge is read up,
  And ben in politics,
Hand-in-glove, you might say,
  Sence back in '56.

NEVER TALK BACK

NEVER talk back! sich things is repperhensible;
A feller only hurts hisse'f that jaws a man that's hot;
In a quarrel, ef you'll only keep your mouth shet and act sensible,
The man that does the talkin' 'll git worsted every shot!

Never talk back to a feller that's abusin' you—
Jest let him carry on, and rip, and snort, and swear;
And when he finds his blamin' and defamin' 's jest amusin' you,
You've got him clean kaflummixed,—and you want to hold him there!

Never talk back, and wake up the whole com-
munity
And call a man a liar, over Law, er Politics.—
You can lift and land him furder and with grace-
fuller impunity
With one good jolt of silence than half a dozen
kicks!

"A BRAVE REFRAIN"

WHEN snow is here, and the trees look weird,
  And the knuckled twigs are gloved with frost;
When the breath congeals in the drover's beard,
  And the old pathway to the barn is lost;
When the rooster's crow is sad to hear,
  And the stamp of the stabled horse is vain,
And the tone of the cow-bell grieves the ear—
  O then is the time for a brave refrain!

When the gears hang stiff on the harness-peg,
  And the tallow gleams in frozen streaks;
And the old hen stands on a lonesome leg,
  And the pump sounds hoarse and the handle
    squeaks;

When the woodpile lies in a shrouded heap,
  And the frost is scratched from the window-
    pane,
And anxious eyes from the inside peep—
  O then is the time for a brave refrain!

When the ax-helve warms at the chimney-jamb!
  And hob-nailed shoes on the hearth below,
And the house-cat curls in a slumber calm,
  And the eight-day clock ticks loud and slow;

When the harsh broom-handle jabs the ceil
  'Neath the kitchen-loft, and the drowsy brain
Sniffs the breath of the morning meal—
  O then is the time for a brave refrain!

ENVOI.

When the skillet seethes, and a-blubbering hot
Tilts the lid of the coffee-pot,
And the scent of the buckwheat cake grows
    plain—
O then is the time for a brave refrain!

ME AND MARY

ALL my feelin's in the Spring
    Gits so blame contrary,
I can't think of anything
    Only me and Mary!
"Me and Mary!" all the time,
"Me and Mary!" like a rhyme,
Keeps a-dingin' on till I'm
    Sick o' "Me and Mary!"

"Me and Mary! Ef us two
    Only was together—
Playin' like we used to do
    In the Aprile weather!"
All the night and all the day
I keep wishin' thataway
Till I'm gittin' old and gray
Jes on "Me and Mary!"

Muddy yit along the pike
    Sence the Winter's freezin',
And the orchard's back'ard-like
    Bloomin' out this season;
Only heerd one bluebird yit—
Nary robin ner tomtit;
What's the how and why of it?
    'Spect it's "Me and Mary!"

Me and Mary liked the birds—
    That is, *Mary* sorto'
Liked 'em first, and afterwards,
    W'y, I thought *I'd* ort'o.
And them birds—ef Mary stood
Right here with me, like she should—
They'd be singin', them birds would,
    All fer me and Mary.

Birds er not, I'm hopin' some
    I can git to plowin'!
Ef the sun'll only come,
    And the Lord allowin',

Guess to-morry I'll turn in
And git down to work ag'in;
This here loaferin' won't win,
    Not fer me and Mary!

Fer a man that loves like me,
    And's afeard to name it,
Till some other feller, he
    Gits the girl—dad-shame-it!
Wet er dry, er clouds er sun—
Winter gone er jes begun—
Outdoor work fer me er none,
    No more "Me and Mary!"

FIRE AT NIGHT

Fɪʀᴇ! Fire! Ring! and ring!
Hear the old bell bang and ding!
Fire! Fire! 'way at night,—
Can't you hear?—I think you might!—

Can't you hear them-air clangin' bells?—
W'y, *I* can't hear nothin' else!
Fire! Ain't you 'wake at last!—
Hear them horses poundin' past—

Hear that ladder-wagon grind
Round the corner!—and, behind,
Hear the hose-cart, turnin' short,
And the horses slip and snort,
As the engine's clank-and-jar
Jolts the whole street, near and far.
Fire! Fire! Fire! Fire!
Can't you hist that winder higher?
La! they've all got past like "scat!"
Night's as black as my old hat—
And it's rainin', too, at that! . . .
Wonder where their old fire's at!

A FALL CRICK VIEW OF THE EARTHQUAKE

I kin hump my back and take the rain,
  And I don't keer how she pours;
I kin keep kindo' ca'm in a thunder-storm,
  No matter how loud she roars;
I hain't much skeered o' the lightnin'
  Ner I hain't sich awful shakes
Afeard o' *cyclones*—but I don't want none
  O' yer dad-burned old earthquakes!

As long as my legs keeps stiddy,
  And long as my head keeps plum',
And the buildin' stays in the front lot,
  I still kin whistle, *some!*

But about the time the old clock
  Flops off'n the mantel-shelf,
And the bureau skoots fer the kitchen,
  I'm a-goin' to skoot, myself!

Plague-take! ef you keep me stabled
  While any earthquakes is around!—
I'm jist like the stock,—I'll beller
  And break fer the open ground!

And I 'low you'd be as nervous,
  And in jist about my fix,
When yer whole farm slides from inunder you,
  And on'y the mor'gage sticks!

Now cars hain't a-goin' to kill you
  Ef you don't drive 'crost the track;
Crediters never'll jerk you up
  Ef you go and pay 'em back;
You kin stand all moral and mundane storms
  Ef you'll on'y jist behave—
But a' EARTHQUAKE:—well, ef it wanted you
  It 'ud husk you out o' yer grave!

MR. SILBERBERG

AND LITTLE JULIUS

I LIKE me yet dot leedle chile
  Vich climb my lap up in to-day,
  Unt took my cheap cigair avay,
Unt laugh and kiss me purty-whvile,—

Possescially I like dose mout'
Vich taste his moder's like—unt so,
Eef my cigair it gone clean out
—Yust let it go!

Vat I caire den for anyding?
Der "HERALDT" schlip out fon my handt
Unt all my odvairtizement standt
Mitout new changements boddering;
I only t'ink—I have me dis
Von leedle boy to pet unt love
Unt play me vit, unt hug unt kiss—
Unt dot's enough!

Der plans unt pairposes I vear
Out in der vorld all fades avay,
Unt vit der beeznis of der day
I got me den no time to spare;
Der caires of trade vas caires no more—
Dem cash accounts dey dodge me by,
Unt vit my chile I roll der floor,
Unt laugh unt gry!

Ach! frient! dem childens is der ones
  Dot got some happy times—you bet!—
  Dot 's vy ven I been growed up yet
I visht I shtill been leedle vonce!
  Unt ven dot leedle roozter tries
    Dem baby-tricks I used to do,
  My mout it vater, unt my eyes
    Dey vater too!

Unt all der summertime unt spring
  Of childhood it come back to me,
  So dot it vas a dream I see
Ven I yust look at anyding!
  Unt ven dot leedle boy run by,
  I dink "Dot's me," fon hour to hour
  Schtill chasing yet dose butterfly
    Fon flower to flower!

Oxpose I vas lots money vairt,
  Mit blenty schtone-front schtore to rent,
  Unt mor'gages at twelf per tcent.,
Unt diamonds in my ruffled shairt,—

I make a'signment of all dot,
  Unt tairn it over mit a schmile
Aber you please—but, don'd forgot,
  I keep dot chile!

SPIRITS AT HOME

THE FAMILY

There was Father, and Mother, and Emmy, and
Jane,
And Lou, and Ellen, and John and me—
And father was killed in the war, and Lou
She died of consumption, and John did too,
And Emmy she went with the pleurisy.

THE SPIRITS

Father believed in 'em all his life—
But Mother, at first, she'd shake her head—
Till after the battle of Champion Hill,
When many a flag in the winder-sill
Had crape mixed in with the white and red!

I used to doubt 'em myself till then—
  But me and Mother was satisfied
When Ellen she set, and Father came
And rapped "God Bless You!" and Mother's
    name,
  And "The flag's up here!" And we just all
    cried.

Used to come often, after that,
  And talk to us—just as he used to do,
Pleasantest kind! And once, for John,
He said he was "lonesome but wouldn't let on—
  Fear mother would worry, and Emmy and
    Lou."

But Lou was the bravest girl on earth—
  For all she never was hale and strong,
She'd have her fun!—With her voice clean lost
She'd laugh and joke us that "when *she* crossed
  To Father, *we'd* all come taggin' along!"

Died—just that way! And the raps was thick
That night, as they often since occur,
Extry loud! And when *Lou* got back
She said it was Father and her—and "whack!"
She tuck the table—and we knowed *her!*

John and Emmy, in five years more,
Both had went.—And it seemed like fate!—
For the old home *it* burnt down,—but Jane
And me and Ellen we built again
The new house, here, on the old estate.

And a happier family I don't know
Of anywheres—unless it's *them,*—
Father, with all his love for Lou,
And her there with him, and healthy, too,
And laughin', with John and little Em.

And, first we moved in the new house here,
 They all dropped in for a long pow-wow,
"We like your buildin', of course," Lou said,—
"But wouldn't swop with you to save your head—
 For *we* live in the ghost of the old house now!"

A HINT OF SPRING

'Twas but a hint of Spring—for still
The atmosphere was sharp and chill,
Save where the genial sunshine smote
The shoulders of my overcoat,
And o'er the snow beneath my feet
Laid spectral fences down the street.

My shadow even seemed to be
Elate with some new buoyancy,
And bowed and bobbed in my advance
With trippingest extravagance,
And, when the birds chirpt out somewhere,
It seemed to wheel with me and stare.

Above I heard a rasping stir—
And on the roof the carpenter

Was perched, and prodding rusty leaves
From out the choked and dripping eaves—
And some one, hammering about,
Was taking all the windows out.

Old scraps of shingles fell before
The noisy mansion's open door;
And wrangling children raked the yard,
And labored much, and laughed as hard,
And fired the burning trash I smelt
And sniffed again—so good I felt!

LOCKERBIE FAIR

O THE LOCKERBIE FAIR!—Have you heard of its
fame
And its fabulous riches, too rare for a name!—
The gold of the noon of the June-time refined
To the Orient-Night, till the eyes and the mind
Are dazed with the sights, in the earth and the
air,
Of the opulent splendors of Lockerbie Fair.

What more fortunate fate might to mortal befall,
Midst the midsummer beauty and bloom of it all,
Than to beam with the moon o'er the rapturous
scene
And twink with the stars as they laughingly lean
O'er the luminous revel and glamour and glare
Fused in one dazzling glory at Lockerbie Fair.

The Night, like a queen in her purple and lace,
With her diamonded brow, and imperious grace
As she leads her fair votaries, train upon train,
A-dance thro' the feasts of this mystic domain
To the mandolin's twang, and the warble and
blare
Of voice, flute and bugle at Lockerbie Fair.

All strange, ever-changing, enchanted delights
Found now in this newer Arabian Nights,—
Where each lovely maid is a Princess, and each
Lucky swain an Aladdin—all treasures in reach
Of the lamps and the rings—and with Genii to
spare,
Simply waiting your orders, at Lockerbie Fair.

A TINKLE OF BELLS

THE LIGHT of the moon on the white of the
snow,
And the answering twinkles along the street,
And our sleigh flashing by, in the glamour and
glow
Of the glorious nights of the long ago,
When the laugh of her lips rang clear and sweet
As the tinkle our horses shook out of the bells
And flung and tossed back
On our glittering track
In a shower of tremulous, murmuring swells
Of the echoing, airy, melodious bells!—
O the mirth of the bells!
And the worth of the bells!
Come tinkle again, in this dearth of the bells,—
This laughter and love that I lack, yearning back,
For the far-away sound of the bells!

Ah! the bells, they were glad in the long ago!
And the tinkles they had, they have thrilled me so
I have said: "It is they and her songs and face
Make summer for me in the wintriest place!"
  And now—but sobbings and sad farewells,
  As I peer in the night through the sleeted pane,
Hearing a clangor and wrangle of bells,
  And never a tinkle again!

The snow is a-swoon, and the moon dead-white,
And the frost is wild in the air to-night!
  Yet still will I linger and listen and pray
  Till the sound of her voice shall come this way,
    With a tinkle of bells,
      And the lisp-like tread
        Of the hooves of the sleigh,
  And the murmurs and swells
    Of the vows she said.
And O, I shall listen as madmen may,
Till the tinkling bells ring down this way!—

Till again the grasp of my hand entwines
The tensioned loops of the quivering lines,
And again we ride in the wake of the pride
And the strength of the coursers, side by side;
With our faces smitten again by the spray
Of the froth of our streets as we gallop away
  In affright of the bells,
And the infinite glee and delight of the bells,
As they tinkle and tinkle and tinkle, till they
Are heard through a dawn where the mists are
    drawn,
And we canter a gallop and dash away
  Sheer into The Judgment Day!

AN OLD FRIEND

HEY, Old Midsummer! are you here again,
With all your harvest-store of olden joys,—
Vast overhanging meadow-lands of rain,

And drowsy dawns, and noons when golden grain
Nods in the sun, and lazy truant boys
Drift ever listlessly adown the day,
Too full of joy to rest, and dreams to play.

The same old Summer, with the same old smile
Beaming upon us in the same old way

We knew in childhood! Though a weary while
Since that far time, yet memories reconcile
The heart with odorous breaths of clover-
hay;
And again I hear the doves, and the sun streams
through
The old barn-door just as it used to do.

And so it seems like welcoming a friend—
An old, *old* friend, upon his coming home
From some far country—coming home to spend
Long, loitering days with me: And I extend
My hand in rapturous glee:—And so you've
come!—
Ho, I'm so glad! Come in and take a chair:
Well, this is just like *old* times, I declare!

MY BACHELOR CHUM

O a corpulent man is my bachelor chum,
  With a neck apoplectic and thick—
An abdomen on him as big as a drum,
  And a fist big enough for the stick;
With a walk that for grace is clear out of the case,
  And a wobble uncertain—as though
His little bow-legs had forgotten the pace
  That in youth used to favor him so.

He is forty, at least; and the top of his head
  Is a bald and a glittering thing;
And his nose and his two chubby cheeks are as
    red
  As three rival roses in Spring.

His mouth is a grin with the corners tucked in,
  And his laugh is so breezy and bright
That it ripples his features and dimples his chin
  With a billowy look of delight.

He is fond of declaring he "don't care a straw"—
  That "the ills of a bachelor's life
Are blisses compared with a mother-in-law,
  And a boarding-school miss for a wife!"
So he smokes and he drinks, and he jokes and he
    winks,
  And he dines and he wines, all alone,
With a thumb ever ready to snap as he thinks
  Of the comforts he never has known.

But up in his den—(Ah, my bachelor chum!)—
  I have sat with him there in the gloom,
When the laugh of his lips died away to become
  But a phantom of mirth in the room.

And to look on him there you would love him,
for all
His ridiculous ways, and be dumb
As the little girl-face that smiles down from the
wall
On the tears of my bachelor chum.

HER BEAUTIFUL HANDS

O YOUR HANDS—they are strangely fair!
Fair—for the jewels that sparkle there,—
Fair—for the witchery of the spell
That ivory keys alone can tell;
But when their delicate touches rest
Here in my own do I love them best,
As I clasp with eager, acquisitive spans
My glorious treasure of beautiful hands!

Marvelous—wonderful—beautiful hands!
They can coax roses to bloom in the strands
Of your brown tresses; and ribbons will twine,
Under mysterious touches of thine,
Into such knots as entangle the soul
And fetter the heart under such a control
As only the strength of my love understands—
My passionate love for your beautiful hands.

As I remember the first fair touch
Of those beautiful hands that I love so much,
I seem to thrill as I then was thrilled,
Kissing the glove that I found unfilled—
When I met your gaze, and the queenly bow,
As you said to me, laughingly, "Keep it
now!" . . .
And dazed and alone in a dream I stand,
Kissing this ghost of your beautiful hand.

When first I loved, in the long ago,
And held your hand as I told you so—
Pressed and caressed it and gave it a kiss
And said "I could die for a hand like this!"
Little I dreamed love's fullness yet
Had to ripen when eyes were wet
And prayers were vain in their wild demands
For one warm touch of your beautiful hands.

Beautiful Hands!—O Beautiful Hands!
Could you reach out of the alien lands
Where you are lingering, and give me, to-night,
Only a touch—were it ever so light—
My heart were soothed, and my weary brain
Would lull itself into rest again;
For there is no solace the world commands
Like the caress of your beautiful hands.

THE BEST IS GOOD ENOUGH

I QUARREL not with Destiny,
But make the best of everything—
The best is good enough for me.

Leave Discontent alone, and she
Will shut her mouth and let *you* sing.
I quarrel not with Destiny.

I take some things, or let 'em be—
Good gold has always got the ring;
The best is good enough for me.

Since Fate insists on secrecy,
I have no arguments to bring—
I quarrel not with Destiny.

The fellow that goes "haw" for "gee"
Will find he hasn't got full swing.
The best is good enough for me.

ONE only knows our needs, and He
Does all of the distributing.
I quarrel not with Destiny;
The best is good enough for me.

TOIL

He had toiled away for a weary while,
Thro' day's dull glare and the night's deep gloom;
And many a long and lonesome mile
He had paced in the round of his dismal room;
He had fared on hunger—had drank of pain
As the drouthy earth might drink of rain;
And the brow he leaned in his trembling palm
Throbbed with a misery so intense
That never again did it seem that calm
Might come to him with the gracious balm
Of old-time languor and indolence.
And he said, "I will leave the tale half told,
And leave the song for the winds to sing;
And the pen—that pitiless blade of gold
That stabs my heart like a dagger-sting—
I will drive to the hilt through the inkstand's top
And spill its blood to the last black drop!"

Then he masked his voice with a laugh, and went
Out in the world with a lawless grace—
With a brazen lie in his eyes and face
Told in a smile of glad content:
He roved the rounds of pleasure through,
And tasted each as it pleased him to;
He joined old songs, and the clink and din
Of the revelers at the banquet hall;
And he tripped his feet where the violin
Spun its waltz for the carnival;
He looked, bedazed, on the luring wile
And the siren-light of a woman's smile,
And peered in her eyes as a diver might
Peer in the sea ere he leaps from sight,—
Caught his breath, with a glance above,
And dropped full-length in the depths of love.

* * * * * * * * * *

'Tis well if ever the false lights die
On the alien coasts where our wreck'd hopes lie!
'Tis well to feel, through the blinding rain,
Our outflung hands touch earth again!

So the castaway came, safe from doom,
Back at last to his lonely room
Filled with its treasure of work to do
And radiant with the light and bloom
Of the summer sun and his glad soul, too!
And sweet as ever the song of birds,
Over his work he sang these words:—

"O friends are good, with their princely ways,
And royal hearts they are goodly things;
And fellowship, in the long dark days
When the drear soul cowers with drooping wings,
Is a thing to yearn for.—*Mirth* is good,—
For a ringing laugh is a rhythmic cry
Blown like a hail from the Angelhood
To the barque of the lone soul drifting by.—
Goodly, too, is the mute caress
Of woman's hands and their tenderness—
The warm breath wet with the dews of love—
The vine-like arms, and the fruit thereof—
The touch that thrills, and the kiss that melts,—
But Toil is sweeter than all things else."

HIS ROOM

"I'm home again, my dear old Room,
I'm home again, and happy, too,
As, peering through the brightening gloom,
I find myself alone with you:
Though brief my stay, nor far away,
I missed you—missed you night and day—
As wildly yearned for you as now.—
Old Room, how are you, anyhow?

"My easy chair, with open arms,
Awaits me just within the door;
The littered carpet's woven charms
Have never seemed so bright before,—
The old rosettes and mignonettes
And ivy-leaves and violets,
Look up as pure and fresh of hue
As though baptized in morning dew.

"Old Room, to me your homely walls
Fold round me like the arms of love,
And over all my being falls
A blessing pure as from above—
Even as a nestling child caressed
And lulled upon a loving breast,
With folded eyes, too glad to weep
And yet too sad for dreams or sleep.

"You've been so kind to me, old Room—
So patient in your tender care,
My drooping heart in fullest bloom
Has blossomed for you unaware;
And who but you had cared to woo
A heart so dark, and heavy too,
As in the past you lifted mine
From out the shadow to the shine?

"For I was but a wayward boy
When first you gladly welcomed me
And taught me work was truer joy
Than rioting incessantly:

And thus the din that stormed within
The old guitar and violin
Has fallen in a fainter tone
And sweeter, for your sake alone.

"Though in my absence I have stood
In festal halls a favored guest,
I missed, in this old quietude,
My worthy work and worthy rest—
By *this* I know that long ago
You loved me first, and told me so
In art's mute eloquence of speech
The voice of praise may never reach.

"For lips and eyes in truth's disguise
Confuse the faces of my friends,
Till old affection's fondest ties
I find unraveling at the ends;
But as I turn to you, and learn
To meet my griefs with less concern,
Your love seems all I have to keep
Me smiling lest I needs must weep.

"Yet I am happy, and would fain
  Forget the world and all its woes;
So set me to my tasks again,
  Old Room, and lull me to repose:
    And as we glide adown the tide
    Of dreams, forever side by side,
    I'll hold your hands as lovers do
    Their sweethearts' and talk love to you."

THE PATHS OF PEACE

MAURICE THOMPSON—FEBRUARY 14, 1901

HE would have holiday—outworn, in sooth,
  Would turn again to seek the old release,—
The open fields—the loved haunts of his youth—
  The woods, the waters, and the paths of peace.

The rest—the recreation he would choose
  Be his abidingly! Long has he served
And greatly—ay, and greatly let us use
  Our grief, and yield him nobly as deserved.

Perchance—with subtler senses than our own
  And love exceeding ours—he listens thus
To ever nearer, clearer pipings blown
  From out the lost lands of Theocritus.

Or, haply, he is beckoned from us here,
By knight or yeoman of the bosky wood,
Or, chained in roses, haled a prisoner
Before the blithe Immortal, Robin Hood.

Or, mayhap, Chaucer signals, and with him
And his rare fellows he goes pilgriming;
Or Walton signs him, o'er the morning brim
Of misty waters midst the dales of Spring.

Ho! wheresoe'r he goes, or whosoe'er
He fares with, he has bravely earned the boon.
Be his the open, and the glory there
Of April-buds, May-blooms and flowers of June!

Be his the glittering dawn, the twinkling dew,
The breathless pool or gush of laughing streams—
Be his the triumph of the coming true
Of all his loveliest dreams!

IN STATE

Is IT the martins or katydids?—
  Early morning or late at night?
A dream, belike, kneeling down on the lids
  Of a dying man's eyesight.

. . . .

Over and over I heard the rain—
  Over and over I waked to see
The blaze of the lamp as again and again
  Its stare insulted me.

. . . .

It is not the click of the clock I hear—
  It is the *pulse* of the clock,—and lo!
How it throbs and throbs on the quickened ear
  Of the dead man listening so!

I heard them whisper She would not come;
  But, being dead, I knew—I knew!
Some hearts they love us alive, and some
  They love us dead—they do!

And I am dead—and I joy to be,—
  For here are my folded hands, so cold
And yet blood-warm with the roses she
  Has given me to hold.

Dead—yea, dead!—But I hear the beat
  Of her heart as her warm lips touch my brow—
And O how sweet—how blinding sweet
  To know that she loves me *now!*

THE MUTE SINGER

I

THE morning sun seemed fair as though
It were a great red rose ablow
In lavish bloom,
With all the air for its perfume,—
Yet he who had been wont to sing,
Could trill no thing.

II

Supine, at noon, as he looked up
Into the vast inverted cup
Of heavenly gold,
Brimmed with its marvels manifold,
And his eye kindled, and his cheek—
Song could not speak.

III

Night fell forebodingly; he knew
Soon must the rain be falling, too,—
And, home, heartsore,
A missive met him at the door—
—Then Song lit on his lips, and he
Sang gloriously.

THE TRIBUTE OF HIS HOME

BENJAMIN HARRISON, INDIANAPOLIS,
MARCH 14, 1901

Bowed, midst a universal grief that makes
  Columbia's self a stricken mourner, cast
  In tears beneath the old Flag at half-mast,
A sense of glory rouses us and breaks
Like song upon our sorrowing and shakes
  The dew from our drenched eyes, that smile at last
  In childish pride—as though the great man passed
To his most high reward for our poor sakes.

Loved of all men—we muse,—yet ours he was—
Choice of the Nation's mighty brotherhood—
Her soldier, statesman, ruler.—Ay, but then,
We knew him—long before the world's applause
And after—as a neighbor, kind and good,
Our common friend and fellow-citizen.

EDGAR WILSON NYE

OBIT FEBRUARY 22, 1896

The saddest silence falls when Laughter lays
Finger on lip, and falteringly breaks
The glad voice into dying minor shakes
And quavers, lorn as airs the wind-harp plays
At wane of drearest Winter's bleakest days.
A troubled hush, in which all hope forsakes
Us, and the yearning upstrained vision aches
With tears that drown e'en heaven from our gaze.
Such silence—after such glad merriment!
O prince of halest humor, wit and cheer!
Could you speak yet to us, I doubt not we
Should catch your voice, still blithely eloquent
Above all murmurings of sorrow here,
Calling your love back to us laughingly.

SONGS OF A LIFE-TIME

MRS. SARAH T. BOLTON'S POEMS

1897

Songs of a Life-Time—with the Singer's head
A silvery glory shining midst the green
Of laurel-leaves that bind a brow serene
And godlike as was ever garlanded.—
So seems *her* glory who herein has wed
Melodious Beauty to the strong of mien
And kingly Speech—made kinglier by this queen
In lilied cadence voiced and raimented.
Songs of a Life-Time: by your own sweet stress
Of singing were ye loved of bygone years—
As through our day ye are, and shall be hence,
Till *fame divine* marks your melodiousness
And on the Singer's lips, with smiles and tears,
Seals there the kiss of love and reverence.

A NOON INTERVAL

A DEEP, delicious hush in earth and sky—
A gracious lull—since, from its wakening,
The morn has been a feverish, restless thing
In which the pulse of Summer ran too high
And riotous, as though its heart went nigh
To bursting with delights past uttering:
Now, as an o'erjoyed child may cease to sing
All falteringly at play, with drowsy eye
Draining the pictures of a fairy-tale
To brim his dreams with—there comes o'er the day
A loathful silence, wherein all sounds fail
Like loitering tones of some faint roundelay . . .
No wakeful effort longer may avail—
The wand waves, and the dozer sinks away.

OLD HEC'S IDOLATRY

HEIGH-O! our jolly tilts at New World song!—
What was the poem indeed! and where the
bard—
"Stabbing his inkpot ever, not his heart,"
As Hector phrased it contumeliously,
Mouthing and munching, at the orchard-stile,
A water-cored rambo whose spirted juice
Glanced, sprayed and flecked the sunlight as he
mouth'd
And muncht, and muncht and mouth'd. All loved
the man!
"Our Hector" as his *Alma Mater* oozed
It into utterance—"Old Hec" said we
Who knew him, hide-and-tallow, hoof-and-horn!
So he: "O ay! my soul! our New World song—
The tweedle-deedles of our modern school—

A school of minnows,—not one gamy bass—
To hook the angler, not the angler him.
Here! all ye little fishes: tweedle-dee!
Soh! one—along the vasty stream of time—
Glints to the surface with a gasp,—and, lo,
A bubble! and he thinks, 'My eye!—see there,
Ye little fishes,—there's a song I've sung!'
Another gapes: another bubble; then
He thinks: 'Well, is it not a wondrous art
To breathe a great immortal poem like that!'
And then another—and another still—
And yet another,—till from brim to brim
The tide is postuled over with a pest
Of bubbles—bursting bubbles! Ay! O ay!"
So, bluff old Hec. And we, who knew his mood
Had ramped its worst—unless we roused it yet
To ire's horriffickest insanity
By some inane, unguarded reference
To "verse beragged in Hoosier dialect"—
(A strangely unforgotten coinage of
Old Hec's long years agone)—we, so, forbore

A word, each glimpsing each, as down we sank,
Couched limply in the orchard's selvage, where—
The rambo finished and the soggy core
Zippt at a sapphire wasp with waist more slim
Than any slender lady's, of old wars,
Pent fasting for long sennights in tall towers
That overtop the undercringing seas—
With one accordant voice, the while he creased
His scroll of manuscript, we said, "Go on."
Then Hector thus:

AN IDYLL OF THE KING

Erewhile, at Autumn, to King Arthur's court
Came Raelus, clamoring: "Lo, has our house
Been sacked and pillaged by a lawless band
Of robber knaves, led on by Alstanés,
The Night-Flower named, because of her fair
face,
All like a lily gleaming in the dusk

Of her dark hair—and like a lily brimmed
With dewy eyes that drip their limpid smiles
Like poison out, for by them has been wro't
My elder brother's doom, as much I fear.
While three days gone was holden harvest-feast

At Lynion Castle—clinging like a gull
High up the gray cliffs of Caerleon—
Came, leaf-like lifted from the plain below
As by a twisted wind, a rustling pack

Of bandit pillagers, with Alstanés
Bright-fluttering like a red leaf in the front.
And ere we were aware of fell intent—
Not knowing whether it was friend or foe—
We found us in their toils, and all the house
In place of guests held only prisoners—
Save that the host, my brother, wro't upon
By the strange beauty of the robber queen,
Was left unfettered, but by silken threads
Of fine-spun flatteries and wanton smiles
Of the enchantress, till her villain thieves
Had rifled as they willed and signal given
To get to horse again. And so they went—
Their leader flinging backward, as she rode,
A kiss to my mad brother—mad since then,—
For from that sorry hour he but talked
Of Alstanés, and her rare beauty, and
Her purity—ay, even that he said
Was star-white, and should light his life with
love
Or leave him groping blindly in its quest

Thro' all eternity. So, sighing, he
Went wandering about till set of sun,
Then got to horse, and bade us all farewell;
And with his glamoured eyes bent trancedly

Upon the tumbled sands that marked the way
The robber-woman went, he turned and chased
His long black shadow o'er the edge of night."—
So Raelus, all seemingly befret

With such concern as nipped his utterance
In scraps of speech: at which Sir Lancelot,
Lifting a slow smile to the King, and then
Turning his cool eye on the youth—"And you
Would track this siren-robber to her hold
And rout her rascal followers, and free
Your brother from the meshes of this queen
Of hearts—for there you doubtless think him?"
"Ay!"
Foamed Raelus, cheek flushed and eye aflame,—
"So even have I tracked, and found them, too,
And know their burrow, shrouded in a copse,
Where, faring in my brother's quest, I heard
The nicker of his horse, and followed on,
And found him tethered in a thicket wild,
As tangled in its tress of leaf and limb
As is a madman's hair; and down the path
That parted it and ran across a knoll
And dipped again, all suddenly I came
Upon a cave, wide-yawning 'neath a beard
Of tangled moss and vine, whence issuing

I heard, blown o'er my senses faint and clear
As whiffs of summer wind, my brother's voice
Lilting a love-song, with the burden tricked
With dainty warblings of a woman's tongue:
And even as I listening bent, I heard
Such peals of wanton merriment as made
My own heart flutter as a bird that beats
For freedom at the bars that prison it.
So turned I then and fled as one who flies
To save himself alone—forgetful of all
Of that my dearer self—my brother.—O!"—
Breaking as sharply as the icy blade
That loosens from the eave to slice the air
And splinter into scales of flying frost—
"Thy help! Thy help! A dozen goodly knights—
Ay, even that, if so it be their hearts
Are hungry as my own to right the wrong!"

So Raelus. And Arthur graciously
Gave ear to him, and, patient, heard him thro',
And pitied him, and granted all he asked;

Then took his hand and held it, saying, "Strong
And ever stronger may its grasp be knit
About the sword that flashes in the cause
Of good."
Thus Raelus, on the morrow's front,
Trapped like a knight and shining like a star,
Pranced from the archway of the court, and led

His glittering lances down the gleaming road
That river-like ran winding till it slipped
Out of the palace view and spilled their shields
Like twinkling bubbles o'er the mountain brim.
Then happed it that as Raelus rode, his tongue
Kept even pace and cantered ever on
Right merrily. His brother, as he said,
Had such an idle soul within his breast—
Such shallowness of fancy for his heart
To drift about in—that he well believed
Its anchor would lay hold on any smile
The lees of womanhood might offer him.
As for himself, he loved his brother well,
Yet had far liefer see him stark and white
In marble death than that his veins shuld burn
With such vitality as spent its flame
So garishly it knew no steady blaze,
But ever wavered round as veered the wind
Of his conceit; for he had made his boast—
Tho' to his own shame did he speak of it—
That with a wink he could buy every smile

That virtue owned. So tattled Raelus
Till, heated with his theme, he lifted voice
And sang the song, "The Light of Woman's
Eyes!"

"O bright is gleaming morn on mountain height;
And bright the moon, slipt from its sheath of night,—
But brighter is the light of woman's eyes.

"And bright the dewdrop, trembling on the lip
Of some red rose, or lily petal-tip,
Or lash of pink,—but brighter woman's eyes.

"Bright is the firefly's ever-drifting spark
That throbs its pulse of light out in the dark;
And bright the stars,—but brighter woman's eyes.

"Bright morn or even; bright or moon or star,
And all the many twinkling lights that are,—
O brighter than ye all are woman's eyes."

So Raelus sang.—And they who rode with him
Bewildered were, and even as he sang
Went straggling, twos and threes, and fell behind
To whisper wonderingly, "Is he a fool?"
And "Does he waver in his mind?" and "Does
The newness of adventure dazzle him?"
So spake they each to each, till far beyond,
With but one loathful knight in company,
They saw him quit the beaten track, and turn
Into the grassy margin of a wood.
And loitering, they fell in mocking jest
Of their strange leader! "See! why, see!" said
    one,—
"He needs no help to fight his hornets' nest,
But one brave knight to squire him!"—pointing
    on
To where fared on the two and disappeared.
"O ay!" said one, "belike he is some old
War-battered knight of long-forgotten age,
That, bursting from his chrysalis, the grave,
Comes back to show us tricks we never dreamed!"

"Or haply," said another, with a laugh,—
"He rides ahead to tell them that he comes
And shrive them ere his courage catches up."
And merry made they all, and each in turn
Filliped a witty pellet at his head:
Until, at last, their shadows shrunk away
And shortened 'neath them and the hour was
noon.
They flung them from their horses listlessly
Within the grassy margin of the wood
Where had passed Raelus an hour agone:
And, hungered, spied a rustic; and they sent
To have them such refreshment as might be
Found at the nearest farm,—where, as it chanced,
Was had most wholesome meat, and milk, and
bread;
And honey, too, celled in its fretted vase
Of gummy gold and dripping nectar-sweet
As dreamed-of kisses from the lips of love;
Wine, too, was broughten, rosy as the dawn
That ushers in the morning of the heart;

And tawny, mellow pear, whose golden ore
Fell molten on the tongue and oozed away
In creamy and delicious nothingness;
And netted melon, musky as the breath
Of breezes blown from out the Orient;
And purple clusterings of plum and grape,
Blurred with a dust dissolving at the touch,
Like flakes the fairies had snowed over them.
And as the idlers basked, with toast and song
And graceful dalliance and wanton jest,
A sound of trampling hooves and jingling reins
Brake sudden, stilled them; and from out a dim
Path leading from the bosky wood there came
A troop of mounted damsels, nigh a score,
Led by a queenly girl, in crimson clad,
With lissome figure lithe and willowy,
And face as fair and sweet and pure withal
As might a maiden lily-blossom be
Ere it has learned the sin of perfect bloom:
Her hair, blown backward like a silken scarf
And fondled by the sun, was glossier

And bluer black than any raven's wing.
"And O!" she laughed, not knowing she was
heard
By any but her fellows: "Men are fools!"
Then drawing rein, and wheeling suddenly,
Her charger mincing backward,—"Raelus—
My Raelus is greater than ye all,
Since he is such a fool that he forgets
He is a man, and lets his tongue of love
Run babbling like a silly child's; and, pah!
I puff him to the winds like thistle-down!"
And, wheeling as she spake, found staring up,
Wide-eyed and wondering, a group of knights,
Half lifted, as their elbows propped their heads,
Half lying; and one, smirker than the rest,
Stood bowing very low, with upturned eyes
Lit with a twinkling smile: "Fair lady—and
Most gracious gentlewoman"—seeing that
The others drew them back as tho' abashed
And veiled their faces with all modesty,
Tho' she, their leader, showed not any qualm,—

"Since all unwittingly we overheard
Your latest speech, and since we know at last
'All men are fools,' right glad indeed am I
That such a nest of us remains for you
To vanquish with those eyes." Then, serious,
That she nor smiled nor winced, nor anything—
"Your pardon will be to me as a shower
Of gracious rain unto a panting drouth."
So bowed in humblest reverence; at which
The damsel, turning to her followers,
Laughed musically,—"See! he proves my
 words!"
Whereat the others joined with inward glee
Her pealing mirth; and in the merriment
The knights chimed, too, and he, the vanquished
 one,
Till all the wood rang as at hunting-tide
When bugle-rumors float about the air
And echoes leap and revel in delight.

Then spake the vanquished knight, with mental
eye
Sweeping the vantage-ground that chance had
gained,—
"Your further pardon, lady. Since the name
Of Raelus fell from those lips of thine,
We fain would know of him. He led us here,
And as he went the way wherefrom your path
Emerges, haply you may tell us where
He may be found?"
"What! Raelus?" she cried,—
"He comes with you?—The brave Sir Raelus?—
That mighty champion?—that gallant knight?—
That peerless wonder of all nobleness?
Then proud am I to greet ye, knowing that;
And, certes, had I known of it ere now,
Then had I proffered you more courtesy
And told you, ere the asking, that he bides
The coming of his friends a league from this,

Hard by a reedy mere, where in high tune
We left him singing, nigh an hour agone."
Then, as she lightly wheeled her horse about
And signal gave to her companions
To follow, gaily cried: "Tell Raelus
His cousin sends to him her sad farewells
And fond regrets, and kisses many as
His valorous deeds are numbered in her heart."
And with "Fair morrow to ye, gentle knights!"
Her steed's hooves struck the highway at a
    bound;
And dimly thro' the dust they saw her lead
Her fluttering cavalcade as recklessly
As might a queen of Araby, fleet-horsed,
Skim o'er the level sands of Syria;
So vanished. And the knights with one accord
Put foot in stirrup, and, with puzzled minds
And many-channeled marvelings, filed in
The woody path, and fared them on and on
Thro' denser glooms, and ways more intricate;

Till, mystified at last and wholly lost,
They made full halt, and would have turned them
back
But that a sudden voice brake on their ears
All piteous and wailing, as distressed:
And, following these cries, they sharply came
Upon an open road that circled round
A reedy flat and sodden tract of sedge,
Moated with stagnant water, crusted thick
With slimy moss, wherein were wriggling things
Entangled, and blind bubbles bulging up
And bursting where from middle way upshot
A tree-trunk, with its gnarled and warty hands
As tho' upheld to clutch at sliding snakes
Or nip the wet wings of the dragon-fly.
Here gazing, lo! they saw their comrade, he
That had gone on with Raelus; and he
Was tugging to fling back into its place
A heavy log that once had spanned the pool

And made a footway to the sedgy flat
Whence came the bitter wailing cries they heard.

Then hastened they to join him in his task;
But, panting, as they asked of Raelus,
All winded with his work, yet jollier
Than meadow-lark at morn, he sent his voice
In such a twittering of merriment,
The wail of sorrow died and laughter strewed
Its grave with melody.

"O Raelus!
Rare Raelus!" he cried and clapped his hands,
And even in the weeds that edged the pool
Fell wrestling with his mirth.—"Why, Raelus,"
He said, when he at last could speak again,
"Drew magnet-like—you know that talk of his,—
And so, adhesive, did I cling and cling
Until I found us in your far advance,
And, hidden in the wood, I stayed to say
'Twas better we should bide your coming. 'No.'
Then on again; and still a second time—
'Shall we not bide their coming?' 'No!' he said;
And on again, until the third; and 'No—
We'll push a little further.' As we did;
And, sudden, came upon an open glade—
There to the northward,—by a thicket bound:
Then he dismounted, giving me his rein,
And, charging me to keep myself concealed,
And if he were not back a certain time
To ride for you and search where he had gone,
He crossed the opening and passed from sight

Within the thicket. I was curious:
And so, dismounting, tethered our two steeds
And followed him; and, creeping warily,
Came on him where—unseen of him—I saw
Him pause before the cave himself described
Before us yesternoon. And here he put
His fingers to his lips and gave a call
Bird-like and quavering: at which a face,
As radiant as summer sun at morn,
Parted the viny curtains of the cave;
And then, a moment later, came in view
A woman even fairer than my sight
Might understand. 'What! dare you come
    again?'
As, lifting up her eyes all flashingly,
She scorched him with a look of hate.—'Begone!
Or have you—traitor, villain, knave, and cur,—
Bro't minions of the law to carry out
The vengeance of your whimpering jealousy?'
Then Raelus, all cowering before
Her queenly anger, faltered: 'Hear me yet;

I do not threaten. But your love—love!—
O give me that. I know you pure as dew:
Your love! Your love!—The smile that has gone
    out
And left my soul a midnight of despair!—
Your love or life! For I have even now
Your stronghold girt about with certain doom
If you but waver in your choice.—Your love!'
At which, as quick as tho't, leapt on him there
A strong man from the covert of the gloom;
And others, like to him, from here and there
Came scurrying. I, turning, would have fled,
But found myself as suddenly beset
And tied and tumbled there with Raelus.
And him they haltered by his squirming heels
Until he did confess such villainy
As made me wonder if his wits were sound—
Confessed himself a renegade—a thief—
Ay, even one of them, save that he knew
Not that nice honor even thieves may claim
Among themselves.—And so ran on thro' such

A catalogue of littlenesses, I
For deafest shame had even stopped my ears
But that my wrists were lockt. And when he
came
To his confession of his lie at court,
By which was gained our knightly sympathy
And valiant service on this fools' crusade,
I seemed to feel the redness of my blush
Soak thro' my very soul. There I brake in:
'Fair lady and most gallant,—to my shame
Do I admit we have been duped by such
An ingrate as this bundled lump of flesh
That I am helpless to rise up and spurn:
Unbind me, and I promise such amends
As knightly hands may deign to wreak upon
A thing so vile as he.' Then, laughing, she:
'First tell me, by your honor, where await
Your knightly brothers and my enemies.'
To which I answered, truthfully, I knew
Not where you lingered, but not close at hand
I was assured. Then all abrupt, she turned:

'Get every one within! We ride at once!'
And scarce a dozen minutes ere they came
Outpouring from the cave in such a guise
As made me smile from very wonderment.—
From head to heel in woman's dress they came,
Clad richly, too, and trapped and tricked withal
As maidenly, but in the face and hand,
As ever damsels flock at holiday.
Then were their chargers bro't, caparisoned
In keeping; and they mounted, lifting us,
Still bounden, with much jest and mockery
Of soft caress and wanton blandishments,
As tho' they were of sex their dress declared.
And so they carried us until they came
Upon the road there as it nicks the copse;
And so drew rein, dismounted, leaving some
To guard their horses; hurried us across
This footway to the middle of the flat.
Here Raelus was bounden to a tree,
Stript to the waist; my fetters cut, and then
A long, keen switch put in my hand, and 'Strike!

Strike as all duty bids you!' said the queen.
And so I did, with right good will at first;
Till, softened as I heard the wretch's prayers
Of anguish, I at last withheld my hand.

'What! tiring?' chirpt the queen: 'Give me the
stick!'
And swish, and swish, and mercy how it rained!

Then all the others, forming circlewise,
Danced round and round the howling wretch, and
jeered
And japed at him, and mocked and scoffed at
him,
And spat upon him. And I turned away
And hid my face; then raised it pleadingly:
Nor would they listen my appeal for him;
But left him so, and thonged and took me back
Across the mere, and drew the bridge, that none
Might go to him, and carried me with them
Far on their way, and freed me once again;
And back I turned, tho' loath, to succor him."
And even as he ceased they heard the wail
Break out anew, and crossed without a word,
And Raelus they found, and without word
They loosed him. And he brake away and ran
As runs a lie the truth is hard upon.

Thus did it fare with Raelus. And they
Who knew of it said naught at court of it,
Nor from that day spake ever of him once,
Nor heard of him again, nor cared to hear.

UNLESS

WHO has not wanted does not guess
  What plenty is.—Who has not groped
In depths of doubt and hopelessness
  Has never truly hoped.—
Unless, sometimes, a shadow falls
  Upon his mirth, and veils his sight,
  And from the darkness drifts the light
    Of love at intervals.

And that most dear of everything,
  I hold, is love; and who can sit
With lightest heart, and laugh and sing,
  Knows not the worth of it.—
Unless, in some strange throng, perchance,
  He feels how thrilling sweet it is,
  One yearning look that answers his—
    The troth of glance and glance.

Who knows not pain, knows not, alas!
  What pleasure is.—Who knows not of
The bitter cup that will not pass,
  Knows not the taste of love.
O souls that thirst, and hearts that fast,
  And natures faint with famishing,
  God lift and lead and safely bring
    You to your own at last!

PROSE OR VERSE?

PROSE or Verse—or Verse or Prose?
Ever thus the query goes,—
Which delight do we prefer—
Which the finer—daintier?

Each incites a zest that grows—
Prose or Verse—or Verse or Prose?—
Each a lotus-eater's spell
Wholly irresistible.

All that wit may fashion, free-
Voiced, or piped in melody,—
Prose or Verse—or Verse or Prose—
Which of these the mastery knows?

'Twere as wise to question, friend—
As of this alluring blend,—
The aroma or the rose?—
Prose or Verse—or Verse or Prose?

"GO READ YOUR BOOK!"

How many times that grim old phrase
Has silenced me, in childish days!
    And *now*—as then it did—
The phantom admonition, clear
And dominant, rings,—and I hear,
    And do as I am bid.

"Go read your book!" my good old sire
Commanded, in affected ire,
    When I, with querying look
And speech, dared vex his studious mind
With idle words of any kind.—
    And so I read my book.

Though seldom, in that *wisest* age,
Did I discern on Wisdom's page
    More than the *task:* that led

At least to *thinking,* and at last
To reading less, and not so fast,
    And longing as I read.

And, lo! in gracious time, I grew
To love a book all through and through!—
    With yearning eyes I look
On any volume,—old, maybe,
Or new—'tis meat and drink to me.—
    And so I read my book.

Old dog-eared Readers, scarred and inked
With school-boy hatred, long extinct;—
    Old Histories that bored
Me worst of all the school;—old, worn
Arithmetics, frayed, ripped, and torn—
    Now Ye are all adored!

And likewise I revere and praise
My sire, as now, with vainest gaze
    And hearing, still I look

For the old face so grave yet dear—
Nay, still I *see,* and still I *hear!*
 And so I read my book.

Next even to my nearest kin,—
My wife—my children romping in
 From school to ride my knee,—
I love a book, and dispossess
My lap of it with loathfulness,
 For all their love of me.

For, grave or gay the book, it takes
Me as an equal—calms, or makes
 Me, laughing, overlook
My little self—forgetful all
Of being so exceeding small.
 And so I read my book.